David and Goliath

Published in Nashville, Tennessee, by Oliver-Nelson Books, a division of Thomas
Nelson, Inc., Publishers, and distributed in Canada by Lawson Falle, Ltd.,
Cambridge, Ontario.

ISBN 0-8407-3416-6

Manufactured in Singapore.

1 2 3 4 5 6 7 — 97 96 95 94 93 92

David and Goliath

Halcyon Backhouse

Illustrated by
Stephen Walsh

A Division of Thomas Nelson Publishers
Nashville

When David was a boy, he had a job.
He looked after his dad's sheep.
Lions and bears were in the hills.
But David was a good shot
with his sling.
And God helped him keep
the sheep safe.

The country was at war.
And the enemy was close
to David's farm.
David had three big brothers.
They went off to fight
for King Saul.

David's dad said,
"Take this bread and cheese
to your brothers.
See how they are getting
along in the army."

Goliath came out from
the enemy lines.
He was a giant.
He was over nine feet tall.
He yelled out,
"Pick a man to fight me.
Go on! I dare you!
The one who wins,
wins the war!"

"Oh — er — help!"
said King Saul's men.
"We are in big trouble!"

But David said,
"God is on our side.
What is the reward
if we kill that man?
He does not love God."

David's brother said,
"You pest! Why are you here?
Run home to your sheep."

"I just asked!" David said.
And he went to find King Saul.

"I will fight the giant for you,"
David said.
"And I will kill him."

"How can you?" asked Saul.
"You are just a kid."

"To God, Goliath is nothing,"
said David.
"God saved me from lions and bears.
He will save me from Goliath, too."

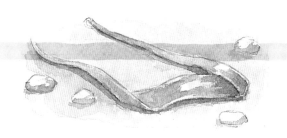

"All right," said Saul.
"You give it a try.
And God go with you."
Saul gave David his
armor and sword.
But they were far too big
for David.

So David did not use them.
He had his stick and his sling.
And he had his trust in God.

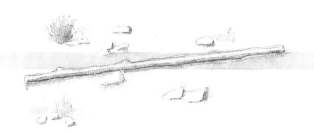

"Ha! Ha!" said Goliath.
"What is that stick for? A dog?
Ha! Ha! Come on,
I will make mush out of you.
Baby face!"

David put a stone in his sling.

Round and round went the sling.
Then zing! Out flew the stone
— and — crash!
Down fell Goliath.
David had won.

"Now the whole world knows.
God saves the people who trust Him,"
David said.